The World of Tapas: 50 Recipes

By: Kelly Johnson

Table of Contents

- Patatas Bravas
- Gambas al Ajillo
- Croquetas de Jamón
- Tortilla Española
- Chorizo al Vino
- Pan con Tomate
- Calamares a la Romana
- Albóndigas
- Piquillos Rellenos de Atún
- Jamón Ibérico
- Pulpo a la Gallega
- Ensaladilla Rusa
- Pinchos Morunos
- Espárragos a la Plancha
- Tzatziki with Pita
- Queso Manchego
- Escalivada
- Berenjenas con Miel
- Ensalada de Pimientos Asados
- Boquerones en Vinagre
- Sopa de Ajo
- Empanadas Gallegas
- Txangurro
- Cordero a la Miel
- Tarta de Santiago
- Piquillos Rellenos de Marisco
- Piquillos Rellenos de Carne
- Gambas a la Plancha
- Tartar de Atún
- Montaditos de Cerdo
- Arroz Negro
- Churros con Chocolate
- Fritura de Pescado
- Salsas: Alioli, Romesco, Mojo Picón
- Mejillones a la Marinera

- Huevos Rotos con Jamón
- Sardinas a la Plancha
- Chistorra
- Ensalada de Tomate con Ventresca
- Piquillos Rellenos de Setas
- Tortillitas de Camarones
- Rabo de Toro
- Gaspacho
- Piquillos con Anchoas
- Morcilla de Burgos
- Setas a la Plancha
- Hummus with Tapenade
- Flamenquín
- Salmorejo
- Pulgas de Jamón

Patatas Bravas

Ingredients:

- 4 large potatoes, peeled and diced
- Olive oil for frying
- 1 tbsp paprika
- 1 tsp garlic powder
- Salt and pepper to taste
- 1 cup tomato sauce
- 1 tbsp chili flakes
- 1 tbsp red wine vinegar

Instructions:

1. Fry the diced potatoes in hot oil until golden and crispy.
2. In a separate pan, cook tomato sauce, chili flakes, paprika, and vinegar.
3. Drizzle the sauce over the fried potatoes and serve.

Gambas al Ajillo

Ingredients:

- 1 lb shrimp, peeled
- 4 garlic cloves, minced
- 1/4 cup olive oil
- 1 tsp red pepper flakes
- Fresh parsley, chopped
- Salt and pepper to taste

Instructions:

1. Heat olive oil in a pan and sauté garlic until fragrant.
2. Add shrimp and red pepper flakes, cooking until the shrimp turns pink.
3. Garnish with fresh parsley and serve.

Croquetas de Jamón

Ingredients:

- 1 cup ham, finely chopped
- 2 cups milk
- 1/2 cup flour
- 1/4 cup butter
- Salt and pepper to taste
- Bread crumbs for coating
- Olive oil for frying

Instructions:

1. Make a béchamel sauce by heating butter, adding flour, and slowly whisking in milk until thickened.
2. Stir in chopped ham and season with salt and pepper.
3. Shape the mixture into small croquettes, coat with breadcrumbs, and fry until golden brown.

Tortilla Española

Ingredients:

- 6 eggs
- 4 large potatoes, peeled and sliced
- 1 onion, sliced
- Olive oil for frying
- Salt and pepper to taste

Instructions:

1. Fry the potatoes and onion in olive oil until tender.
2. Beat the eggs, season with salt and pepper, and pour over the potatoes.
3. Cook until the eggs set, then flip and cook the other side.

Chorizo al Vino

Ingredients:

- 1 lb Spanish chorizo, sliced
- 1/2 cup red wine
- 1 tsp smoked paprika
- Olive oil for frying

Instructions:

1. Fry the chorizo slices in olive oil until crispy.
2. Add red wine and smoked paprika, simmering until the wine reduces.
3. Serve warm.

Pan con Tomate

Ingredients:

- 4 slices rustic bread
- 2 ripe tomatoes, grated
- 2 garlic cloves, halved
- Olive oil
- Salt and pepper

Instructions:

1. Toast the bread slices and rub with garlic.
2. Spread grated tomato on the bread, drizzle with olive oil, and season with salt and pepper.

Calamares a la Romana

Ingredients:

- 1 lb squid, cleaned and sliced into rings
- 1 cup flour
- 1 tsp paprika
- Salt and pepper
- Olive oil for frying

Instructions:

1. Mix flour, paprika, salt, and pepper in a bowl.
2. Coat the squid rings in the flour mixture and fry until golden brown.
3. Serve with lemon wedges.

Albóndigas

Ingredients:

- 1 lb ground beef or pork
- 1/2 cup breadcrumbs
- 1 egg
- 1 tsp garlic, minced
- 1 tbsp parsley, chopped
- Salt and pepper
- Tomato sauce for serving

Instructions:

1. Mix the meat, breadcrumbs, egg, garlic, parsley, salt, and pepper.
2. Form the mixture into meatballs and fry until golden brown.
3. Serve with warm tomato sauce.

Piquillos Rellenos de Atún

Ingredients:

- 12 piquillo peppers, jarred
- 1 can tuna in olive oil
- 1 tbsp mayonnaise
- 1 tbsp parsley, chopped

Instructions:

1. Mix the tuna with mayonnaise and parsley.
2. Stuff the piquillo peppers with the tuna mixture.
3. Serve as a cold tapa.

Jamón Ibérico

Ingredients:

- 12 slices Jamón Ibérico

Instructions:

1. Simply serve the thin slices of Jamón Ibérico on a platter at room temperature.
2. Pair with crusty bread or olives if desired.

Pulpo a la Gallega

Ingredients:

- 1 lb octopus
- 1 tbsp paprika
- 1/4 cup olive oil
- Sea salt to taste
- 1/2 lemon

Instructions:

1. Boil the octopus until tender, about 45 minutes to 1 hour.
2. Slice the octopus and arrange on a plate.
3. Drizzle with olive oil, sprinkle with paprika, and finish with a squeeze of lemon.
4. Serve with crusty bread.

Ensaladilla Rusa

Ingredients:

- 4 medium potatoes, peeled and boiled
- 2 carrots, peeled and boiled
- 1/2 cup peas, boiled
- 1/2 cup mayonnaise
- 1/4 cup olives, chopped
- Salt and pepper to taste

Instructions:

1. Dice the potatoes and carrots.
2. Combine with peas, olives, and mayonnaise in a bowl.
3. Season with salt and pepper.
4. Chill for at least 1 hour before serving.

Pinchos Morunos

Ingredients:

- 1 lb pork or chicken, cubed
- 2 tbsp olive oil
- 1 tsp cumin
- 1 tsp paprika
- 1/2 tsp garlic powder
- Salt and pepper to taste
- Wooden skewers

Instructions:

1. Mix olive oil, cumin, paprika, garlic powder, salt, and pepper.
2. Toss the meat cubes in the marinade and let sit for 30 minutes.
3. Thread the meat onto the skewers and grill until cooked through.
4. Serve with lemon wedges.

Espárragos a la Plancha

Ingredients:

- 1 bunch asparagus, trimmed
- 2 tbsp olive oil
- Salt and pepper
- 1 lemon, sliced

Instructions:

1. Heat a grill or grill pan over medium heat.
2. Toss the asparagus in olive oil and season with salt and pepper.
3. Grill the asparagus for 3-5 minutes until tender and slightly charred.
4. Serve with lemon slices.

Tzatziki with Pita

Ingredients:

- 1 cup Greek yogurt
- 1 cucumber, grated
- 2 tbsp olive oil
- 2 garlic cloves, minced
- 1 tbsp lemon juice
- 1 tbsp fresh dill, chopped
- Salt and pepper to taste
- Pita bread, cut into wedges

Instructions:

1. Combine yogurt, grated cucumber, olive oil, garlic, lemon juice, dill, salt, and pepper.
2. Mix well and chill for 1 hour.
3. Serve with warm pita wedges.

Queso Manchego

Ingredients:

- 1 wedge of Manchego cheese

Instructions:

1. Slice the Manchego cheese thinly.
2. Serve at room temperature with olives or crusty bread.

Escalivada

Ingredients:

- 2 red bell peppers
- 1 eggplant
- 2 onions
- 2 tomatoes
- Olive oil
- Salt and pepper

Instructions:

1. Grill or roast the vegetables (peppers, eggplant, onions, and tomatoes) until charred.
2. Peel the skin off and cut the vegetables into strips.
3. Drizzle with olive oil and season with salt and pepper.
4. Serve chilled or at room temperature.

Berenjenas con Miel

Ingredients:

- 2 eggplants, sliced
- Olive oil for frying
- 1/4 cup honey
- Sea salt

Instructions:

1. Fry the eggplant slices in hot olive oil until golden brown.
2. Drain on paper towels and drizzle with honey.
3. Sprinkle with a pinch of sea salt and serve warm.

Ensalada de Pimientos Asados

Ingredients:

- 3 red bell peppers
- 1/4 cup olive oil
- 1 garlic clove, minced
- 2 tbsp sherry vinegar
- Salt and pepper to taste

Instructions:

1. Roast the peppers until charred, then peel and deseed.
2. Slice the peppers and toss with olive oil, garlic, vinegar, salt, and pepper.
3. Chill for at least 30 minutes before serving.

Boquerones en Vinagre

Ingredients:

- 1 lb fresh anchovies
- 1/2 cup white wine vinegar
- 1/4 cup olive oil
- 2 garlic cloves, minced
- Fresh parsley, chopped
- Salt to taste

Instructions:

1. Clean the anchovies, removing the heads and bones.
2. Marinate the anchovies in vinegar for 1 hour.
3. Drain and drizzle with olive oil, garlic, parsley, and salt.
4. Serve chilled.

Sopa de Ajo

Ingredients:

- 6 cloves garlic, minced
- 4 cups chicken broth
- 2 slices of stale bread
- 2 eggs
- 1/2 tsp paprika
- Olive oil
- Salt and pepper to taste

Instructions:

1. Heat olive oil in a large pot and sauté the garlic until fragrant.
2. Add the chicken broth and bring to a boil.
3. Tear the bread into pieces and add to the broth.
4. Season with paprika, salt, and pepper.
5. Crack the eggs into the soup and cook for a few minutes until they set.
6. Serve hot with a drizzle of olive oil.

Empanadas Gallegas

Ingredients:

- 1 package empanada dough
- 1 lb tuna, drained and flaked
- 1 onion, chopped
- 1 red pepper, chopped
- 1/4 cup olives, chopped
- 1 egg, beaten
- Olive oil
- Salt and pepper

Instructions:

1. Sauté the onion and red pepper in olive oil until soft.
2. Add the tuna, olives, salt, and pepper, and cook for 2-3 minutes.
3. Roll out the empanada dough and spoon the tuna mixture onto one half.
4. Fold over the dough and crimp the edges to seal.
5. Brush with beaten egg and bake at 375°F for 25 minutes until golden brown.

Txangurro

Ingredients:

- 1 lb crab meat
- 1 onion, finely chopped
- 1/2 cup white wine
- 2 tbsp olive oil
- 2 tbsp tomato paste
- 1/4 cup breadcrumbs
- Salt and pepper
- Chopped parsley for garnish

Instructions:

1. Heat olive oil in a pan and sauté the onion until soft.
2. Add the wine and let it reduce.
3. Stir in the tomato paste and crab meat, cooking for a few minutes.
4. Add breadcrumbs to bind the mixture and season with salt and pepper.
5. Spoon into crab shells, garnish with parsley, and serve.

Cordero a la Miel

Ingredients:

- 1 lb lamb chops
- 1/4 cup honey
- 2 tbsp olive oil
- 2 tbsp red wine vinegar
- 2 cloves garlic, minced
- Salt and pepper

Instructions:

1. Mix the honey, olive oil, red wine vinegar, garlic, salt, and pepper.
2. Marinate the lamb chops in the mixture for 1 hour.
3. Grill or pan-fry the lamb chops for 4-5 minutes per side.
4. Serve with a drizzle of the marinade.

Tarta de Santiago

Ingredients:

- 2 cups ground almonds
- 1 cup sugar
- 4 eggs
- 1 tbsp lemon zest
- 1/4 cup flour
- Powdered sugar for dusting

Instructions:

1. Preheat the oven to 350°F.
2. Mix the ground almonds, sugar, eggs, lemon zest, and flour in a bowl.
3. Pour into a greased cake pan and bake for 25-30 minutes.
4. Let cool and dust with powdered sugar before serving.

Piquillos Rellenos de Marisco

Ingredients:

- 12 piquillo peppers, drained
- 1/2 lb shrimp, peeled and chopped
- 1/2 cup bechamel sauce
- 1 tbsp olive oil
- Salt and pepper

Instructions:

1. Sauté the shrimp in olive oil until cooked.
2. Mix the shrimp with bechamel sauce, salt, and pepper.
3. Stuff the piquillo peppers with the shrimp mixture.
4. Serve warm with additional bechamel sauce on top.

Piquillos Rellenos de Carne

Ingredients:

- 12 piquillo peppers
- 1 lb ground beef
- 1 onion, chopped
- 1/2 cup tomato sauce
- 1/4 cup breadcrumbs
- Olive oil
- Salt and pepper

Instructions:

1. Cook the ground beef and onion in olive oil until browned.
2. Add tomato sauce, breadcrumbs, salt, and pepper, and mix well.
3. Stuff the piquillo peppers with the beef mixture.
4. Serve with additional tomato sauce if desired.

Gambas a la Plancha

Ingredients:

- 1 lb shrimp, peeled and deveined
- 2 tbsp olive oil
- 2 cloves garlic, minced
- 1 tbsp lemon juice
- Salt and pepper

Instructions:

1. Heat the olive oil in a pan and sauté the garlic until fragrant.
2. Add the shrimp and cook for 3-4 minutes on each side until pink.
3. Drizzle with lemon juice, season with salt and pepper, and serve.

Tartar de Atún

Ingredients:

- 1 lb fresh tuna, diced
- 1/4 cup olive oil
- 1 tbsp soy sauce
- 1 tbsp sesame oil
- 1 tbsp fresh lime juice
- 1/4 cup cilantro, chopped
- Salt and pepper

Instructions:

1. Combine the tuna, olive oil, soy sauce, sesame oil, lime juice, cilantro, salt, and pepper in a bowl.
2. Mix gently and serve immediately with crackers or toast.

Montaditos de Cerdo

Ingredients:

- 1 lb pork tenderloin, sliced
- 1 tbsp paprika
- 2 tbsp olive oil
- 1 baguette, sliced
- Salt and pepper

Instructions:

1. Season the pork slices with paprika, salt, and pepper.
2. Grill or pan-fry the pork until cooked through.
3. Toast the baguette slices and top each with a slice of pork.
4. Serve as a tapas appetizer.

Arroz Negro (Black Rice)

Ingredients:

- 1 lb squid, cleaned and sliced
- 1/2 lb shrimp, peeled
- 1 onion, finely chopped
- 2 garlic cloves, minced
- 1 red bell pepper, chopped
- 1 1/2 cups short-grain rice
- 4 cups fish or seafood stock
- 1/2 cup white wine
- 1/4 cup olive oil
- 2 tbsp squid ink
- Salt and pepper
- Lemon wedges for serving

Instructions:

1. Heat olive oil in a large paella pan or skillet over medium heat. Add the onion, garlic, and red bell pepper, and sauté until softened.
2. Add the rice and cook for 1-2 minutes, stirring to coat the rice in oil.
3. Pour in the white wine and cook until it evaporates.
4. Add the stock and squid ink, and stir to combine. Season with salt and pepper.
5. Add the squid and shrimp, and cook until the seafood is done and the rice is tender, about 20 minutes. If needed, add more stock or water.
6. Serve with lemon wedges on the side.

Churros con Chocolate

Ingredients:

- 1 cup water
- 1/2 cup butter
- 1 1/2 cups all-purpose flour
- 1/4 tsp salt
- 3 eggs
- 2 tbsp sugar
- Vegetable oil for frying
- 1/2 cup sugar (for coating)
- 1 tsp cinnamon (for coating)
- For chocolate sauce:
    - 4 oz dark chocolate
    - 1/2 cup heavy cream

Instructions:

1. In a saucepan, bring water and butter to a boil. Stir in the flour and salt, and cook for a minute until the dough pulls away from the pan.
2. Remove from heat and mix in the eggs one at a time until smooth. Let cool for 5 minutes.
3. Heat the oil in a deep pan. Spoon the dough into a piping bag fitted with a large star tip.
4. Pipe 4-5 inch long strips into the hot oil and fry until golden brown.
5. Mix sugar and cinnamon in a bowl, then toss the fried churros in the mixture.
6. For the chocolate sauce: Melt the chocolate with cream over low heat until smooth. Serve the churros with the chocolate sauce for dipping.

Fritura de Pescado (Fried Fish)

Ingredients:

- 1 lb white fish fillets (e.g., cod, haddock)
- 1 cup flour
- 1/2 tsp paprika
- Salt and pepper
- Vegetable oil for frying
- Lemon wedges for serving

Instructions:

1. Mix the flour, paprika, salt, and pepper in a shallow bowl.
2. Dredge the fish fillets in the flour mixture, coating evenly.
3. Heat oil in a frying pan over medium-high heat. Fry the fish for 3-4 minutes per side until golden and crispy.
4. Serve with lemon wedges on the side.

Salsas: Alioli, Romesco, Mojo Picón

Alioli (Garlic Mayonnaise Sauce) Ingredients:

- 2 cloves garlic
- 1 egg yolk
- 1 cup olive oil
- 1 tbsp lemon juice
- Salt

Instructions:

1. Crush the garlic in a mortar and pestle, then add a pinch of salt.
2. Gradually whisk in the egg yolk and lemon juice.
3. Slowly add the olive oil, whisking constantly, until the sauce thickens.

Romesco Sauce Ingredients:

- 1 red bell pepper
- 2 tomatoes
- 1/4 cup almonds
- 1 garlic clove
- 1/4 cup olive oil
- 2 tbsp vinegar
- Salt and pepper

Instructions:

1. Roast the bell pepper and tomatoes until charred. Peel the skin off.
2. Blend the roasted vegetables with almonds, garlic, olive oil, vinegar, salt, and pepper until smooth.

Mojo Picón (Canary Islands Sauce) Ingredients:

- 4 cloves garlic
- 1 red chili pepper
- 1/4 cup olive oil
- 2 tbsp vinegar
- 1 tsp cumin
- Salt

Instructions:

1. Blend all ingredients in a food processor until smooth.
2. Adjust seasoning with salt and vinegar to taste.

Mejillones a la Marinera (Mussels in Marinara Sauce)

Ingredients:

- 2 lbs fresh mussels, cleaned
- 1 onion, chopped
- 2 garlic cloves, minced
- 1/2 cup white wine
- 1 can diced tomatoes
- 1 tbsp tomato paste
- 1 tsp paprika
- Olive oil
- Salt and pepper
- Fresh parsley for garnish

Instructions:

1. Heat olive oil in a pan and sauté the onion and garlic until softened.
2. Add the white wine, tomatoes, tomato paste, and paprika. Bring to a simmer.
3. Add the mussels and cover the pan. Cook until the mussels open, about 5 minutes.
4. Garnish with fresh parsley and serve with crusty bread.

Huevos Rotos con Jamón (Broken Eggs with Ham)

Ingredients:

- 4 eggs
- 1/4 lb Jamón Ibérico (or Serrano ham), sliced
- 1 potato, thinly sliced
- Olive oil
- Salt and pepper

Instructions:

1. Fry the potato slices in olive oil until golden and crispy. Remove from the pan and set aside.
2. In the same pan, cook the ham for 2-3 minutes until crispy.
3. In another pan, fry the eggs sunny-side up.
4. Layer the fried potatoes on a plate, top with the crispy ham, and place the eggs on top. Break the eggs to mix with the potatoes.

Sardinas a la Plancha (Grilled Sardines)

Ingredients:

- 12 fresh sardines, cleaned
- Olive oil
- 1 lemon, sliced
- Salt and pepper

Instructions:

1. Preheat the grill to medium-high heat.
2. Drizzle the sardines with olive oil and season with salt and pepper.
3. Grill the sardines for 2-3 minutes on each side until golden and cooked through.
4. Serve with lemon slices.

Chistorra (Spanish Sausage)

Ingredients:

- 1 lb chistorra sausages
- Olive oil

Instructions:

1. Heat olive oil in a pan over medium heat.
2. Cook the chistorra sausages for 5-6 minutes until browned and cooked through.
3. Serve with bread or as an appetizer.

Ensalada de Tomate con Ventresca (Tomato Salad with Tuna Belly)

Ingredients:

- 4 ripe tomatoes, sliced
- 1 can ventresca (tuna belly), drained
- 1/4 red onion, thinly sliced
- Olive oil
- 1 tbsp vinegar
- Salt and pepper
- Fresh basil for garnish

Instructions:

1. Arrange the tomato slices on a plate. Top with slices of onion and the ventresca tuna.
2. Drizzle with olive oil and vinegar. Season with salt and pepper.
3. Garnish with fresh basil and serve.

Piquillos Rellenos de Setas

Ingredients:

- 12 piquillo peppers (jarred or fresh, if available)
- 200g mixed mushrooms (such as button mushrooms, cremini, or wild mushrooms)
- 1 small onion, finely chopped
- 2 cloves garlic, minced
- 2 tablespoons olive oil
- 1/4 cup white wine (optional)
- 1/4 cup breadcrumbs (preferably homemade)
- 2 tablespoons fresh parsley, chopped
- 1 tablespoon sherry vinegar (optional)
- Salt and pepper, to taste
- 1/2 cup bechamel sauce (optional, for extra richness)

Instructions:

1. **Prepare the Piquillo Peppers**: If using jarred piquillo peppers, drain them and carefully remove the seeds. If using fresh piquillo peppers, char them on a grill or under a broiler, then peel off the skin and remove the seeds.
2. **Make the Mushroom Filling**: Heat the olive oil in a pan over medium heat. Add the chopped onion and garlic and sauté for about 5 minutes, until softened. Add the mushrooms, season with salt and pepper, and cook for another 5-7 minutes until the mushrooms release their moisture and begin to brown.
3. **Deglaze and Add Flavor**: Pour in the white wine (if using) and let it cook off for 2-3 minutes. Stir in the breadcrumbs, parsley, and sherry vinegar (if using). Cook for an additional 1-2 minutes until the mixture is thick and well combined. Adjust seasoning with salt and pepper.
4. **Stuff the Peppers**: Carefully stuff each piquillo pepper with the mushroom filling. Arrange the stuffed peppers in a baking dish.
5. **Serve**: If desired, pour a little bechamel sauce over the stuffed peppers for extra creaminess. Bake in a preheated oven at 180°C (350°F) for 10-15 minutes until heated through. Serve warm, garnished with extra parsley.

Tortillitas de Camarones (Shrimp Fritters)

Ingredients:

- 250g small shrimp, peeled and deveined
- 100g chickpea flour (harina de garbanzo)
- 1 small onion, finely chopped
- 1 clove garlic, minced
- 1 teaspoon paprika
- 1/2 teaspoon cumin
- Fresh parsley, chopped
- Salt and pepper to taste
- Water (as needed for batter consistency)
- Olive oil for frying

Instructions:

1. **Prepare the Shrimp**: Chop the shrimp into small pieces. If using larger shrimp, coarsely chop them to ensure they mix well with the batter.
2. **Make the Batter**: In a bowl, combine the chickpea flour, paprika, cumin, and a pinch of salt and pepper. Slowly add water, stirring until you form a thick batter that can hold the shrimp pieces.
3. **Combine Ingredients**: Add the chopped shrimp, garlic, onion, and parsley into the batter. Stir well to coat everything evenly.
4. **Fry the Fritters**: Heat olive oil in a frying pan over medium-high heat. Spoon small dollops of the batter into the pan, flattening them into small pancakes. Fry until golden brown on both sides, about 2-3 minutes per side.
5. **Serve**: Drain on paper towels and serve hot with a wedge of lemon.

Rabo de Toro (Oxtail Stew)

Ingredients:

- 1kg oxtail, cut into pieces
- 2 tablespoons olive oil
- 1 onion, chopped
- 2 carrots, chopped
- 2 cloves garlic, minced
- 1 tomato, chopped
- 1 bottle red wine
- 2 cups beef broth
- 2 bay leaves
- Fresh thyme
- Salt and pepper to taste
- Flour (for dredging)
- Olive oil for browning

Instructions:

1. **Prepare the Oxtail**: Dredge the oxtail pieces in flour and season with salt and pepper. Heat olive oil in a large pot over medium-high heat. Brown the oxtail pieces in batches until they are golden, then set them aside.
2. **Make the Sauce**: In the same pot, sauté the onion, carrots, and garlic until softened. Add the chopped tomato and cook for another 3 minutes.
3. **Simmer**: Return the oxtail to the pot. Pour in the red wine, scraping up any browned bits from the bottom. Add the beef broth, bay leaves, and thyme. Bring to a boil, then reduce to a simmer. Cover and cook for 3-4 hours, or until the oxtail is tender and the meat falls off the bone.
4. **Serve**: Remove the bay leaves and thyme. Serve the stew hot, garnished with fresh herbs or with crusty bread.

Gazpacho (Cold Spanish Tomato Soup)

Ingredients:

- 1kg ripe tomatoes, chopped
- 1 cucumber, peeled and chopped
- 1 bell pepper, chopped
- 1 small onion, chopped
- 2 cloves garlic, minced
- 1/4 cup olive oil
- 2 tablespoons red wine vinegar
- 1/2 teaspoon cumin (optional)
- Salt and pepper to taste
- Water or tomato juice, as needed for consistency

Instructions:

1. **Prepare the Vegetables**: Place the tomatoes, cucumber, bell pepper, onion, and garlic in a blender or food processor. Blend until smooth.
2. **Season the Soup**: Add olive oil, red wine vinegar, cumin (optional), salt, and pepper. Taste and adjust the seasoning as needed.
3. **Chill**: If the soup is too thick, add water or tomato juice to reach your desired consistency. Chill in the refrigerator for at least 1 hour before serving.
4. **Serve**: Pour the gazpacho into bowls, and garnish with a drizzle of olive oil or chopped fresh herbs, if desired.

Piquillos con Anchoas (Piquillo Peppers with Anchovies)

Ingredients:

- 12 piquillo peppers (jarred or fresh)
- 12 anchovy fillets (packed in oil)
- 2 tablespoons extra virgin olive oil
- 1 tablespoon red wine vinegar
- Fresh parsley, chopped (for garnish)
- Salt and pepper, to taste

Instructions:

1. **Prepare the Piquillo Peppers**: If using jarred piquillo peppers, drain and carefully remove any seeds. If using fresh peppers, char them over a grill or under a broiler, peel off the skin, and remove the seeds.
2. **Stuff the Peppers**: Gently stuff each piquillo pepper with an anchovy fillet.
3. **Serve**: Arrange the stuffed peppers on a plate. Drizzle with olive oil and red wine vinegar, and sprinkle with chopped parsley. Serve as a tapa or appetizer.

Morcilla de Burgos (Burgos Blood Sausage)

Ingredients:

- 500g morcilla de Burgos (blood sausage)
- 1 tablespoon olive oil
- 1 onion, finely chopped
- 1/2 cup red wine
- Fresh parsley, chopped (for garnish)

Instructions:

1. **Cook the Morcilla**: Heat the olive oil in a frying pan over medium heat. Add the morcilla sausages and cook, turning occasionally, until browned and heated through, about 5-7 minutes.
2. **Prepare the Onion Sauce**: In the same pan, add the chopped onion and sauté until softened. Add the red wine and cook for 3-4 minutes, allowing the sauce to reduce.
3. **Serve**: Slice the morcilla into rounds and serve with the onion sauce. Garnish with fresh parsley.

Setas a la Plancha (Grilled Mushrooms)

Ingredients:

- 500g mixed mushrooms (such as cremini, portobello, or shiitake)
- 2 tablespoons olive oil
- 2 cloves garlic, minced
- Fresh thyme or parsley, chopped
- Salt and pepper, to taste
- Lemon wedges (for serving)

Instructions:

1. **Prepare the Mushrooms**: Clean the mushrooms by wiping them with a damp cloth. Slice large mushrooms into thick pieces, leaving smaller ones whole.
2. **Grill the Mushrooms**: Heat the olive oil in a grill pan or large skillet over medium-high heat. Add the mushrooms and cook for 4-5 minutes per side until they are tender and have grill marks.
3. **Serve**: Sprinkle with garlic, fresh herbs, salt, and pepper. Serve with lemon wedges for a fresh touch.

Hummus with Tapenade

Ingredients for Hummus:

- 1 can (400g) chickpeas, drained and rinsed
- 2 tablespoons tahini
- 2 tablespoons olive oil
- 1 clove garlic, minced
- 2 tablespoons lemon juice
- Salt and pepper, to taste

Ingredients for Tapenade:

- 100g Kalamata olives, pitted
- 1 tablespoon capers
- 1 clove garlic
- 2 tablespoons olive oil
- 1 tablespoon lemon juice

Instructions:

1. **Make the Hummus**: In a food processor, combine the chickpeas, tahini, olive oil, garlic, lemon juice, salt, and pepper. Blend until smooth, adding water as needed to reach the desired consistency.
2. **Make the Tapenade**: In a blender or food processor, combine the olives, capers, garlic, olive oil, and lemon juice. Pulse until the mixture is finely chopped but still slightly chunky.
3. **Serve**: Spoon the hummus into a bowl and top with the tapenade. Serve with pita, crackers, or fresh vegetables.

Flamenquín

Ingredients:

- 4 pork tenderloin cutlets, thinly sliced
- 4 slices serrano ham
- 1 egg, beaten
- 1 cup flour
- 1 cup breadcrumbs
- Olive oil for frying
- Salt and pepper, to taste

Instructions:

1. **Prepare the Flamenquín**: Place a slice of serrano ham on each piece of pork. Roll them up tightly and secure with toothpicks.
2. **Breading**: Dredge each roll in flour, dip in beaten egg, and coat with breadcrumbs.
3. **Fry the Flamenquín**: Heat olive oil in a frying pan over medium heat. Fry the rolls until golden brown and cooked through, about 4-5 minutes per side.
4. **Serve**: Remove the toothpicks and serve hot, often accompanied by French fries or a simple salad.

Salmorejo

Ingredients:

- 1kg ripe tomatoes, chopped
- 150g stale white bread, crust removed
- 1/4 cup extra virgin olive oil
- 2 tablespoons sherry vinegar
- 1 clove garlic, minced
- Salt, to taste
- Hard-boiled eggs, chopped (for garnish)
- Jamón ibérico, finely chopped (for garnish)

Instructions:

1. **Blend the Ingredients**: In a blender, combine the tomatoes, bread, garlic, olive oil, vinegar, and salt. Blend until smooth and thick.
2. **Chill**: Refrigerate the salmorejo for at least 1 hour.
3. **Serve**: Pour into bowls and garnish with chopped hard-boiled eggs and jamón ibérico. Serve cold.

Pulgas de Jamón (Ham Rolls)

Ingredients:

- 12 small baguette rolls (or crusty bread)
- 12 slices jamón ibérico or serrano ham
- 1 tablespoon olive oil
- 1/2 cup fresh arugula or rocket (optional)

Instructions:

1. **Prepare the Rolls**: Slice the baguette rolls in half. Drizzle a little olive oil on the inside of each roll.
2. **Assemble the Pulgas**: Place a slice of ham inside each roll and top with fresh arugula, if using.
3. **Serve**: Close the rolls and serve immediately as a delicious Spanish tapa or snack.